PAST & PRESENT

MILFORD

OPPOSITE: This c. 1908 photograph shows what will become one of the US Treasury building's 55-ton columns sitting on a railcar at the quarry of the Lovejoy Granite Company. Thirty-one of these columns in all were quarried from the Lovejoy quarry. Today, the quarry is filled with water and is privately owned. One side of the large quarry operates as an event venue called Stonehaven Events, LLC. (Courtesy of Milford Historical Society.)

MILFORD

Christopher Thompson and Sara Weyant-Bunn

To our dear friend Roberta Douglas. Her dedication to researching, preserving, and sharing Milford's history was an inspiration.

Copyright © 2023 by Christopher Thompson and Sara Weyant-Bunn
ISBN 978-1-4671-0901-7

Library of Congress Control Number: 2022940317

Published by Arcadia Publishing
Charleston, South Carolina

Printed in the United States of America

For all general information, please contact Arcadia Publishing:
Telephone 843-853-2070
Fax 843-853-0044
E-mail sales@arcadiapublishing.com
For customer service and orders:
Toll-Free 1-888-313-2665

Visit us on the Internet at www.arcadiapublishing.com

ON THE FRONT COVER: This past image was shot around 1910 and about 40 years after the land called "the Oval" actually became more of a triangle. The massive elm trees seen on the south side of the common mark the original perimeter of the pre-1870 Oval. Many will also notice the Pillsbury Bandstand sitting in its original location, more in the middle of the common. It sat there from 1896 until 1927, when it was moved to its current home to make room for the World War I Memorial. (Both, courtesy of the Milford Historical Society.)

ON THE BACK COVER: One of two double-arch stone bridges over the Souhegan River in Milford, the one pictured was originally built in 1846. Eighty-five years later, in 1931, the bridge was widened from about 19 feet to 35 feet to accommodate the increasing traffic from automobiles and trucks. At 176 years old, Milford's stone bridge has been and continues to be a key roadway connecting Union Square to points north of the river. (Courtesy of Milford Historical Society.)

CONTENTS

ACKNOWLEDGMENTS

The authors would like to acknowledge all current and past members of the Milford Historical Society. For more than 125 years, these volunteers' dedication to preserving Milford's history made this book possible. Special thanks go to our current board of directors for their support of this endeavor. They are Mark Genovesi, Roberta Douglas, Barbara Tortorelli, Greg White, Karl Dahlen, Charlie Annand, Denise Fox, Walter Friesendorf, Dave Nelson, and the authors. Milford's Wadleigh Memorial Library must also be acknowledged for its preservation work. It offers an online and searchable collection of the archives of the *Milford Cabinet*, Milford's weekly local newspaper since 1802. Much of the history told in this book comes from the *Milford Cabinet* online archive. All of the historical images contained in this publication are courtesy of the Milford Historical Society. All present-day images are courtesy of the authors.

Thanks to our families for putting up with our early mornings and late evenings sitting at the computer, either doing research or trying to make sure the vantage of a particular image is just right. Thanks for supporting us in our many missions around town to get the shot under just the right weather conditions. We came to envy the photographers of the earlier images as they didn't have to deal with today's volume of traffic. There were many images that required us to stand in the middle of a busy street to get the shot.

Christopher Thompson would like to thank his daughter Taylor and her boyfriend, Nat, for letting him use their Canon DSLR camera for many of the pictures he contributed—and thanks to Sara for educating him on how to use it, as taking pictures with his four-year-old cell phone camera just didn't get the job done. We have to acknowledge Jordan Greenberg for providing us with rooftop access to a couple of downtown buildings to get the correct vantage and then a second time to get the shot when the weather conditions were just right.

INTRODUCTION

Over 150 years of Milford, New Hampshire's history are included in this publication. Milford's first 70 years of existence were before the age of photography. Years ago, before cameras, Milford and surrounding towns were small New England communities where everyone knew everyone. Most families had their own farm, growing their own food and raising livestock. Families were large because many hands were needed to maintain the family farm. Primitive one-room schoolhouses existed for the education of Milford's children; a few of these schoolhouses still exist today as private residences. Today's forests marked with antique stone walls were once rolling meadows filled with livestock and gardens. Many of the roads traveled today in shiny automobiles were just rough trails or gravel pathways traveled by horse and two-wheeled carriages. Farmers would bring their lumber and harvested grains to Milford's lumber and gristmills for processing. Residents would travel to town to attend religious services or conduct business. Aside from rough sketches and drawings, it is sometimes hard to imagine what Milford looked like in its first 70 years before photography.

Fortunately, with the invention and common use of cameras in the mid-19th century, a great visual picture of Milford at an earlier time is available. The images show not only how it has changed but also how many aspects have remained the same. Milford is often described as the quintessential small New England town, with a traditional downtown area complete with a grassed common and 19th-century bandstand. This downtown area is known on maps as Union Square, but locals have called it "the Oval" for generations. Many images contained in this publication come from the Oval, the unofficial heart of Milford. In addition to images of the Oval, scenes from all around town are included to show both areas that have changed significantly and those that remain similar to the past.

Some of the earliest photographs of Milford known to exist come from the 1860s, when Union Square looked considerably different than it does today. With the construction of a new Town House in 1869 (which remains our town hall today), many of the buildings on or around Union Square needed to be moved or removed from the area. Eagle Hall was turned 90 degrees clockwise and physically moved about 125 feet to the northeast to where it sits today. Other buildings were moved to create Middle Street. Winifred "Winnie" Wright documented a lot of these building moves and even drew a map in her 1979 publication, *The Granite Town: Milford, New Hampshire, 1901–1978*. With Eagle Hall moved, the town opted to enlarge the Oval to the size it remains today. Aside from a few building changes on the south and west side of Union Square, a lot of what came to be in 1869–1870 remains very similar today.

Milford's Union Square and downtown area have seen many improvements over the past 35 years thanks to dedicated citizens and their love of Milford. In 1988, several committees were formed to decide what to do about the town hall. The building and its infrastructure were in need of repairs due to numerous fire and safety problems. The town hall restoration efforts led to the creation of the Milford Pumpkin Festival in 1990 to raise money to save the building. Thanks to these citizens' efforts, Milford's town hall is now in the National Register of Historic Places. The Downtown Ongoing Improvement Team (DO-IT), created in 1992, took on a number of projects to better Milford's character. It continued to coordinate the annual Pumpkin Festival, and its efforts led to Milford receiving the Great American Main Street award in 2002. DO-IT eventually became the Milford Improvement Team (MIT) and continued to coordinate the Pumpkin Festival until 2017. With the future of the Pumpkin Festival in jeopardy, 2018 saw a true grass-roots effort by local citizens to rescue the 28-year-old annual tradition, and so was born the Granite Town Festivities Committee to continue the Pumpkin Festival tradition.

Milford's citizens are passionate about their town and its traditions. Thanks to all of the aforementioned teams and committees and their volunteers for their efforts in keeping Milford the place people come to call home.

CHAPTER 1

AROUND THE OVAL

On the weekend of August 16, 1946, a huge "Welcome Home" celebration was held to honor the sacrifices made by Milford's servicemen and women during World War II. The celebration included a parade through the Oval, complete with four bands, sixty-five floats, and a formation of the recently returned service members.

The image below shows the Milford Town Hall before the $15,000 library annex was built in 1892. Originally containing 4,000 books, the library collection had grown to over 6,700 volumes by 1899. The dedication ceremony on June 28, 1892, included an orchestra and speeches from leading citizens. The upper story of the annex was leased by the Masonic fraternity. This building housed Milford's library until 1950.

The Lull fountain at the Wadleigh Library was originally the gift of Mary Lull, the widow of Col. Oliver Lull, who was killed in the Civil War. It sat on the grounds of their home, where the library sits today. Her intent was for the fountain to be a symbol of the reuniting of America after the Civil War. When the library was built in 1950, the fountain was re-established on the grounds, and it has undergone much restoration since.

These images capture the buildings at Nos. 1 and 19 Nashua Street. The east-most floor space of No. 1 Nashua Street was occupied by Holt Brothers Meats & Provisions when this older image was taken. From 1912 until 1966, this space served as the restaurants of George Hatch, Arnold Wheaton, and Walter Philbrick. Walter Philbrick's restaurant occupied this space for 40 years. The building was heavily remodeled in 2018 and is decorated for the 2021 Milford Pumpkin Festival in the image below.

In 1891, William B. Rotch, publisher of the *Farmer's Cabinet*, purchased the newspapers the *Milford Advance* and *Wilton Journal*. He combined these three newspapers into the *Milford Cabinet* and moved its operation to the Melzar Block in Milford. In 1893, he bought this building at the intersection of Elm and Union Streets, where it was published until the operation moved to the former Brick School building in 1951.

The image below, taken in the late 1960s, shows the south side of Union Square at the time. Aside from the vintage automobiles, some of the vintage businesses here are Darling's Gift Shop, Dyer's Drugs, News Stand, and Wright Fashions. Dyer Drugs went out of business in the mid-1990s after 65 years of doing business on the Oval. Today, the building that housed Darlings and Dyers is home to Café on the Oval and has been since 2012.

James Shanahan erected this building around 1869 and used the south half of the first floor for his shoe repair business. When this photograph was taken in the 1890s, D.C. Raymond was the shoe dealer. He was later succeeded by M.P. Cullinan. In the north half, Frank W. Richardson operated a successful men's clothing store. Around 1917, the spaces were combined, and for decades, it was the home of the popular Boulter Drug Store.

From 1949 until 1981, this building on Middle Street housed Ray Gagnon's Western Auto Associate Store, and it has housed a number of businesses both before and after. Originally known as the Oyster Saloon, the building was turned 90 degrees and moved about 100 feet to the east around the time the Milford Town Hall was built in 1869. The building originally sat on the east side of Union Square and faced west.

AROUND THE OVAL

William Crosby's two-story house was constructed before Milford's incorporation in 1794 and originally stood where the Milford Town Hall is today. Around 1850, the building was raised to its present three-story height. It was moved in 1869 to make room for the new Milford Town Hall. Since that time, it has been divided into two spaces and has been the site of many retail and service businesses.

Today, and for many years the home of Union Street Grill, this building at 4 Union Street has a long history. Originally built by Dr. Simeon Stickney on his South Street land about 1865, it became home to Emerson's furniture store in 1881. The Emersons outgrew their space and sold the building to Lydia and John Melendy. In 1895, the Melendys had it moved to where it stands today.

From 1857 until 1892, the Jacques Block (left) operated as Milford's fire station. In 1915, William Jacques operated a shoe repair business and store here. He added the third story in 1923. His son carried on the business until 1972. The Canary Block (right), once a bright-yellow wood building, burned down in 1929. John Flanagan reconstructed it in 1931 and leased it to various businesses. Andre Vincent purchased it in 1962 and used it for his beauty shop.

These images show the buildings on the north side of Middle Street. Middle Street was created in 1869 when the Milford Town Hall was built. The building that today serves as the Olde Kilkenny Pub on the corner of Putnam Street has a long history. From 1873 until 1912, it served as a blacksmith shop. It also served as a theater for a few decades. Permattach Diamond Tool Company was here from 1954 until 1964. Kilkenny's was started here in 2000.

The Foster Block, named for its first owner, Benjamin Foster, was built in 1890. Described by the *Farmer's Cabinet* newspaper as being "admirably located for business purposes," the west half of the building housed his auctioneer and undertaking businesses. He rented out the east half of the building to various businesses, including Webster's Pharmacy. In 1946, Army veteran James Cassidy bought the building, remodeled the top two floors into eight apartments, and named it after two children in his family, the Peter Carol Apartments.

The image below was likely taken during Milford's Industrial Carnival in October 1911. It shows the west side of Union Square. Many of these buildings were heavily damaged by fire on October 7, 1929. The fire started in the basement of the second building from the left and spread to the three-story buildings next to it. The three-story buildings were renovated after the fire and reduced down to the two stories they are today.

Built in 1816 as a Baptist church, this building was moved to its present location in 1836. In 1846, it was expanded by 15 feet, and the spire was added. In 1877, the building was purchased by the Methodist Episcopal church, and it was greatly renovated over the years. The last service in the building was held in July 1985, and the church moved to a new building on North River Road. Today, a music instrument business occupies the space.

In 1904, the Souhegan Bank building was enlarged and the interior and exterior were completely overhauled. The *Milford Cabinet* noted it was "fitted with every convenience for expediting business and labor-saving contrivances," including electric door locks and a vault that weighed over 11 tons. The building was expanded to its present size in 1928, and the interior was refurbished in 1949. Today, it is a popular restaurant that bears the name of the original architect, Luther C. Greenleaf.

Over the years, the Smith Block, built around 1867, housed many businesses, including a tailor shop, bank, barbershop, restaurant, bowling alley, and basketball court. In 1905, C.S. Parker purchased the property, painted it dark olive, and opened the Milford Cash Store, which sold groceries and small provisions. His stock was advertised as "like a running stream—always moving." In 1913, John Smith purchased the building and extended it to build a bowling alley, which operated until 1932.

In 1913, John Smith expanded the basement of his building by 20 feet to accommodate his new bowling alley. Since the expansion extended onto the banks of the Souhegan River, he had to pay rent to the town. The alley opened on December 3 with three lanes. Several leagues and the public enjoyed the alley until it had to be torn down due to the bridge expansion in 1932.

Built in 1842, the Community House was the home of Solomon Livermore, a prominent Milford lawyer. The material and labor for its construction were given in trade for Livermore's legal services. In 1928, the Milford Women's Club undertook the house's restoration, and it has been the meeting place for many local organizations and clubs since. It is still serving this purpose today under the management of the Livermore Community Association.

This side of the Oval is still home to Eagle Hall and several businesses, just as it was when the above photograph was taken in 1885. James Shannahan, who owned the southern block, had a shoe repair business and rented the north half to Frank W. Richardson's clothing store. The middle building housed a meat market owned by Newton Robinson and Charles Kittredge and the Bartlett & Dodge grocery store. The Milford Bookstore occupied the first floor of Eagle Hall.

CHAPTER 2

ON THE ROAD

This house on Federal Hill dates back to before Milford's incorporation. Originally a farm, since 1967, it has been the location of the Mile Away Restaurant. Although expanded and changed by its many owners through the years, original features, such as rough-hewn beams and granite hearths, are still present.

This view from a Milford postcard was taken in front of today's St. Patrick's Church looking toward the junction of Grove and Summer Streets. The first home on the right was built in 1876 by Andrew Fuller and replaced an even older home on the site likely going back to the 18th century. The Catholic Church purchased the property in 1915, and it has since been the church rectory.

AMHERST STREET.   MILFORD. N. H.

The past image here really shows the imposing grand elm trees that once graced the common. Many of them were planted in 1849 and shaded the common and Union Square for generations. They were called wine glass elms because of their graceful shapes and brought much joy and pride to Milford's citizens. A combination of Dutch Elm disease in the 1930s and old age saw the demise of these elm trees throughout the 20th century.

About 130 years separate, these views were taken on South Street in the vicinity of Clinton Street looking north toward Union Square. While several of the homes in view remain today, the one obvious missing feature in the current image is the towering spire of the Baptist church. This particular spire rose about 150 feet from the ground. The church sat where TD Bank sits today and was torn down in 1972 after 98 years of church services.

These images were both taken on Nashua Street between Clinton and High Streets looking toward Union Square. The biggest difference in these images is the asphalt used to smooth today's roads. Many roads in town were macadamized starting in 1905. Before that, dust and mud were daily issues for those traveling the early roads. The constant in these images is the homes. Though remodeling has taken place on some, the homes have changed very little.

In this postcard looking over the Stone Bridge, the streets have remained the same but the buildings north of the bridge have changed. To the left is the back side of the Whittemore Block, razed in 1950 to build a gas station. West of the Whittemore Block was the Riverbank Inn, which was razed in 1939 to construct the post office. South of the Stone Bridge, toward the Oval, has remained almost unchanged since this early postcard was taken.

Union Square, from Mt. Vernon Street, Milford, N. H.

These images were taken on Elm Street looking to the west in the vicinity of the modern-day main entrance to Keyes Field. Like the picture of the elm trees on the common on page 33, this is another image that shows how prominent the elm trees were in Milford and how Elm Street got its name. Like the elms that graced the common, the elms on Elm Street fell victim to old age and Dutch Elm disease.

Even older than the Milford Town Hall, this three-story building on Nashua Street goes back as far as the 1850s. The floor space has always been divided into two separate spaces for businesses to sell their wares. John E. Bruce was the merchant in the west space in the undated photograph above. Today, the building serves the same purpose as it did over 150 years ago, providing spaces for local businesses on the ground floor and apartments on the upper floors.

This brick building on Nashua Street almost across from Clinton Street has been the home of Cardoza Flooring since 2014. Prior to 2014, Cardoza was on the south side of Union Square. The building formerly housed Harland Holt Insurance and Milford's school offices. The large factory building in the earlier picture was in this spot for about 25 years and burned down on December 23, 1905. Its owners used the factory for the manufacture of wood products.

The building to the right in the photograph below is the Whittemore Block, which Prof. W.L. Whittemore operated as both a tenement and a private school. In 1914, he purchased the riverbank land across the street, which was being used as a dumping area. To improve the area, he covered the trash with dirt and planted sunflowers. The building on the left was the Riverbank Inn, which was razed in 1939 to make room for the post office.

These views look down Bridge Street from Union Square between Eagle Hall and the Stone Bridge. Originally called Maple Street, this street that leads down to the swing bridge was changed to Bridge Street in 1948. On the left is the mill building of Morse, Kaley, and Company. The building was completely renovated in the early 1980s and has been known as the Milford Mill Apartments since early 1983.

In 1741, John Shepard built a saw and gristmill at this site on Amherst Street (originally laid out in 1801). In the mid-1800s, the area had expanded to include a cooper and blacksmith shop. The 65-foot chimney stack was added to this complex in 1870. In 1916, due to decay, the chimney was leveled. Hundreds of spectators came to watch W.L. Winslow raze it, toppling 50,000 bricks to within one foot of his intended drop point.

Until 1895, Myrtle Street, shown here, ran south from Adams Street and stopped when it met Billings Street. Residents petitioned the town to construct a bridge and continue Myrtle Street down to Mont Vernon Street. The bridge and road extension was completed in 1895. It was determined a poor job was done on the road construction, and it was completely rebuilt in 1898. The new construction included granite curbing and a sidewalk the entire length of the road.

These images show two very different railings on the Lincoln Street bridge over upper Railroad Pond. The older iron rails were removed from the double-arch granite bridge downtown in 1931 and later installed here on Lincoln Street. They were removed in 1992 when the bridge was rebuilt. Some of this railing is still in use in front of Emerson Park. More forms a border between Union Street Grill and the World War II Memorial Park.

This Rite Aid location on Mont Vernon Street is the original site of the John McLane home, which was razed in 1962. This building took its place and housed Super Save Market, which opened in the autumn of 1962. Super Save became the P&C Market in 1974 and remained in business here until 1989. The image above was taken some time after P&C closed. Wellby Super Drug opened here in 1991, and the location eventually became Brooks and then Rite Aid.

Milford's famed pilot and photographer Bernice Blake Perry snapped this image of Milford Public Works employees paving School Street on October 1, 1954. In March of that year, voters approved the hot top for School Street, but only between Nashua and Middle Streets. The stretch between Middle and Bridge Streets remained unpaved for a period of time. The image below shows what looks like more recent tar between Middle and Bridge Streets.

The small brick building in the foreground of the image below is the original Souhegan Bank building on Nashua Street. It was built about 1854 and was sufficient for conducting the business of banking until 1904, when it became too small and was rebuilt with a bigger footprint. The building was enlarged again in 1928. Today, and since 2019, the remodeled building is home to Greenleaf Restaurant, named after the Boston architect who was responsible for the 1904 redesign.

Since the 18th century, men with their teams of horses would haul fallen trees and their garden harvest to the site of a lumber and gristmill on the corner of Amherst Street just beyond the Stone Bridge. This strip of land along Amherst Street is where the original John Shepherd mill was as early as 1741. The modern building just off the bridge has seen a number of businesses and today hosts Chop Shop Cycles.

CHAPTER 3

AROUND TOWN

Since its earliest inhabitants, dams along the Souhegan River provided power for Milford's industries and directly contributed to the town's evolution. Sawmills, cotton mills, and gristmills depended on the dams for operation and employed most of the town's residents. It is no surprise that water rights were often argued and decided by the courts.

A family reunion takes place at the Elm Street home of Hervey Putnam around 1891. Putnam was born in Wilton in 1820 and lived in Milford for about 50 years. He died at his home at the age of 89 in 1910 and is buried just two lots to the west in the Elm Street Cemetery. The image below was taken in 2021 when the property was decorated for the Pumpkin Festival and Halloween.

AROUND TOWN

The State of New Hampshire purchased this farmland in South Milford off Osgood Road in 1949 and built a garage for the New Hampshire Army National Guard's equipment and as a space to conduct drills. This older garage building can be seen in the above image just beyond the newer armory building. This new and current armory building was erected in 1954, and despite some remodeling over the years, the footprint remains the same.

Burns Rock and Burns Memorial Park sit on Old Brookline Road off of Armory Road. The rock and park were named after John Burns, one of Milford's earliest settlers. Aside from the rock itself, the scenes in these two images are very different. If the modern image had as little vegetation as the older image, in the field behind the rock, one would likely see cars traveling on Route 13 South just to the north of Chappell Tractor.

Benjamin Goodwin built his home with Milford granite some time between 1818 and 1837. It was purchased by Reed Dutton in 1847 and remained in the Dutton family for over 100 years. In the mid-1970s, it was used as an office building. In 2001, it faced demolition, but a fundraising effort from Milford residents saved the structure. Today, it is a residential condominium.

Built as a private residence around 1876 on the north side of Amherst Street, it was reported at the time by the *Farmer's Cabinet* as "one of the most beautiful in the village of Milford, a large commodious residence, with all the modern improvements and latest style of architecture." The home was purchased by the Catholic Church in 1915 and has served as its rectory ever since. St. Patrick's Church sits just to the east of this building.

Around 1892, flag stations were built at Milford's railroad crossings to stop traffic when a train was passing through. Each station was manned by a flagman, who worked out of a small hut that was warmed by a stove. Pictured is Frank Gervais, the flagman at the Union Street crossing. These men landscaped their stations, and in 1904, Frank was awarded a $5 prize by the Boston & Maine Railroad (B&M) for his flower display.

The older image in this series is a rare shot of the footbridge that connected Souhegan Street and Bridge Street before today's swing bridge was built in 1889. The older wooden bridge can also be seen on page 58. The modern bridge was built by the Berlin Iron Bridge Company out of Berlin, Connecticut. The total cost to the Town of Milford for the new bridge in 1889 was about $3,500.

In the above photograph, Bill Medlyn puts the finishing touches on the rock that marks the entrance to the park honoring the Emerson family. The land was willed to the town by Henry Emerson in 1947, and in 1969, a monetary donation came from the children of Charles Emerson (Henry's brother). A true community effort, several local businesses and individuals generously donated funds to complete its development. Today, the park continues to be a much-loved location for residents to enjoy.

Generations of Milford residents have crossed the well-known suspension footbridge, or "swing bridge" as it is called, connecting Bridge and Souhegan Streets. The current bridge was built in 1889 and is in the National Register of Historic Places and the New Hampshire Register of Historic Places. Pictured above is the predecessor to the current swing bridge, which was used between 1869 and 1889.

The photograph below, taken between 1874 and 1895, shows the Melzar Block on the left and Webster Block on the right. For many years, the upper floors of the Melzar Block were a boardinghouse, and the bottom floors were rented to various businesses, including Boynton's tin shop. James Webster's block was built around 1861, and the first floor housed his jewelry store until his sons turned it into an optician shop in 1926. Several different photographers used the upper floor space.

Here one sees the well-known swing bridge that connects Bridge and Souhegan Streets. Each picture features a large building on the Bridge Street side. The earlier image features the French & Heald furniture factory, which burned in 1912.

The modern image features the Granite Square apartments sitting just slightly farther to the west. The apartments were opened in May 1990 and feature 54 apartments.

Today and since 1986, this former train station on South Street has been home to United Auto Body. It was built in 1894 to support the new Fitchburg line. At its peak, this line supported eight trains every day and ran along today's Granite Town Rail Trail. This line was important to Milford's granite industry, as many spur lines were built to haul granite from quarries along this line. The line's last train ran in September 1931.

The First Congregational Church of Milford dedicated its Union Street building on October 1, 1834. It was described by the *Farmer's Cabinet* newspaper as "a neatly finished, convenient and beautiful edifice." The Parish House, just south of the main building, was given to the church in 1863. In the early 1970s, the Parish House was home to Playhouse 101, a live theater organization with visiting professional performers. Both buildings have been improved over the years, but their exteriors have remained close to their original forms.

INDUSTRY
AND SERVICES

A tannery had been located on this site on Elm Street since around 1840. The building pictured was erected in 1885 and was 200 feet long, 75 feet wide, and five stories high. Five hundred employees processed raw hides using hemlock bark and chemicals. The tannery burned down on November 27, 1908.

This shopping center in west Milford held its grand opening on May 8, 1957, to the joy of the citizens of Milford and surrounding towns. Some of the original stores included First National, Godin's, Esquire's Cleaners, and Roy's Radio & TV Service. Mother Daughter Shop, Margaret's Pizza, Devine's Sporting Goods, Slot Car City, Subway, and Blake's Restaurant have been some of the many tenants over the years. The image below was taken in January 1967.

In 1892, the Milford Fire Department moved from the Jacques Block on the west side of the Oval to this basement space in the newly built Milford Town House Annex. Further improvements for the fire department came shortly after the move, when 47 fire hydrants were connected to the town water supply. The fire department continued operations from this location until February 1975, when a new fire station was built on School Street.

Nehemiah Holt, a successful stonecutter and lumber dealer, built his home on Elm Street around 1836. When he died in 1886, it was sold to Henry D. Epps, who enlarged the house and operated it as the Endicott Inn. In addition to a tennis court, the inn boasted a dining room that could seat 60 people. This location continued as an inn until 1915, when it was sold and returned to use as a private home.

After working at Coburn's garage in Milford for 16 years, Alfred "Hank" Medlyn and his wife, Barbara, opened their own auto repair and sales garage in 1961. The Medlyns sold both AMC and Jeep products, and Hank was joined by his sons, Stephen and Ed Medlyn. Though Chrysler pulled the Jeep line in 2009, Medlyn Motors has continued with auto repairs and great service that Milford and the Souhegan Valley have come to expect over their decades of business.

This location at the corner of South and Clinton Streets, where today sits this abandoned gas station, is very historic. Milford's first train station was built here around 1850. That train station building was later moved and today sits at the western corner of Clinton and Franklin Streets and serves as an apartment building. The earlier picture here was probably taken between 1988 and 1991. At the time, Clinton Street was a one-way street running west to east.

INDUSTRY AND SERVICES

Today and for more than 20 years home to Son's Chimney Services, the leftmost building in these Nashua Street images was home to Mike's Store for more than 30 years. World War II Army veteran Felice "Mike" Marchesi owned the building and operated his grocery and meat store here from 1946 until his death in 1979. Well remembered is the walk-in refrigerator door in Mike's store that contained postcards sent from his customers from all over the world.

The newspaper described it as "More Tears Than Cheers" when members of the Signal Corps departed from the Garden Street station on July 27, 1917. They were on their way to North Carolina to quarter while awaiting their overseas assignments to fight in World War I. Seven Milford men died in the war, and a monument honoring their sacrifice was dedicated on the Oval in 1927.

When the Stone Bridge was widened in 1931, this concrete building replaced a wooden structure known as Gilson's Garage. Charles and Owen Fisk bought it in 1934 and operated an electrical shop and gas station. In the 1940s, when the below photograph was taken, Hibbert Miles, a World War II veteran, was the proprietor. On April 1, 1952, it became Bohonan's Auto Service. John Bohonan owned the operation for 27 years. Today, the location is home to a popular full-service motorcycle shop.

In the 1850s, this building on South Street was a storehouse for an iron foundry that produced cooking stoves. After 1857, it was used by Bragg & Conant to make cabinets, mirrors, frames, and fancy boxes. In the early 1900s, the Hawkins Basket Shop occupied the building, where the largest basket in the world was made for the 1911 Milford Industrial Carnival. The Merrimack Farmers Exchange, a cooperative farm supply organization, purchased the building in 1933.

INDUSTRY AND SERVICES

The construction year of the Milford Water Works or Pumping Station, 1889, is still visible in the arch's keystone. The *Milford Cabinet* noted that year as one of "marked advance" to the "material development" of the town. The brick and sandstone exterior has remained virtually unchanged. It was purchased by the town in 1890 and today serves as the headquarters for the Department of Public Works.

In 1913, construction was completed on the Souhegan Auto Company's new showroom. Two stories high, the Nashua Street level had a 2,100-square-foot showroom. The lower level contained the 33-by-78-square-foot storeroom and garage. Adjacent to the main building was the machine shop and forge. Business was brisk, and in 1914, improvements included building a retaining wall and a 100-foot addition to store more autos. Today, this location is home to Cardoza Flooring.

CHAPTER 5

GONE BUT
NOT FORGOTTEN

Hotel Ponemah was built in 1883 close to the site of Milford Springs, water famed for its purity and medicinal qualities. Guests could enjoy dancing to live music, luxurious accommodations, and bowling in the hotel's basement alleys. The owners boasted that due to its elevation, residents would not experience hay fever or mosquitos. The hotel burned down in 1921.

This land and home were purchased by the Town of Milford in July 1893 from Henry Epps. The town then auctioned just the building to M.F. Crosby five months later. Crosby had the building moved about a half mile west to be used as a tenement, and it now sits at 131 Elm Street. In 1894, the town used this lot to build Centennial High School, which served as the high school building until 1961.

Residents always swam at this pool formed by the Great Brook, next to the pumping station, but it was not until 1921 that the area was excavated and a small, sandy beach was added. A bathhouse was constructed, which the boys could use in the morning and the girls in the afternoon. The bathhouse was refurbished and the swimming area expanded in 1951. Due to drought, the area was decommissioned in 1964, and a new pool was built at Keyes Field.

Milford's library has been in this spot on Nashua Street since it was built in 1950. The prior building, known as Lullwood (see page 13), was torn down in the summer of 1949, and site work for the new library began immediately. After 35 years of use, the Wadleigh Library was expanded in 1986 to three times its original size. Ground breaking for the new addition took place in the fall of 1985.

GONE BUT NOT FORGOTTEN

When the Milford Medical Center opened in 1976, the building was already accustomed to having many visitors pass through its doors. In the 1960s, the house served as an official stop for American Youth Hostels. Organized youth groups taking bicycle tours of New England found comfort and hospitality from its owners, Wilfred Mitchell and his wife. Although the interior was completed renovated to provide medical services, the exterior remained unaltered. In 2014, ground was broken for the current facility.

Cumberland Farms, pictured here, was approved and built in 1969 on the former site of the McLane Manufacturing Company, a manufacturer of post office equipment. Prior to 1984, Cumberland Farms was in the west end of the building closest to Pine Street. Gas pumps and a new addition to the building were added in 1984, and Cumberland Farms moved into the new construction. The year 2015 brought another expansion and renovation of Cumberland Farms' retail footprint here on Nashua Street.

GONE BUT NOT FORGOTTEN

Solomon K. Livermore, one of Milford's most respected lawyers, built his law office in 1832. Originally located on Union Street in front of the Congregational church, it was moved to Nashua Street in 1900. It was later purchased by Joseph Rosi and operated as a store selling groceries, general merchandise, and imported goods. In 1927, fire destroyed most of the original building, and only the new addition on the west side remained unscathed. Rosi rebuilt and reopened three months later.

Milford's John McLane served as the governor of New Hampshire from 1905 to 1907. This house on Mont Vernon Street was the McLane home. It had ells on both sides, and the eastern ell can be seen in this image. The western ell was moved in April 1923 and today is the home at 11 Myrtle Street. The home was torn down in 1962 to make room for this commercial building. It has housed many grocery stores and pharmacies.

This building, which once stood on Middle Street, is rumored to have been moved from a nearby location in 1869. Over the years, many businesses operated from the Cascadnac House, including a "working man's" hotel, tailor shop, hardware store, barbershop, residential housing, shoe repair shop, restaurant, tax preparation services, and Operation Help. It was bought by the town in 1993 and razed to open up the bottleneck it caused at the intersection with Putnam Street.

Before the current US Post Office was built on this site, it was the site of the large home pictured below. Eleven different sites around town were considered for the new post office. The home was demolished in June 1939, and construction of the new building began soon thereafter. The new post office building was erected from brick and Milford granite and opened for business on February 1, 1940.

Formerly the site of Fletcher Paint Works, this location on Elm Street was once the site of a blacksmith shop. Owners throughout the years included Grant and Charles Mooar, Edward Finerty, and Wilder Prince. In 1903, Prince installed a gasoline engine that replaced the hand bellows.

That same year, he sold the business to Edward Albee, who expanded the business to include wheelwright work. Albee closed the business in 1916 because the popularity of automobiles reduced the need for blacksmith services.

Exactly 70 years separate, these are pictures of the hill on the west end of Milford once known as the Twin Tows ski area. The ski area was in operation in Milford on what was initially called the Jones Hill slope for 32 years, from 1946 through 1978. The Lions Club ran the operation in its final years. Until no trespassing signs went up in 1986, it served as a great sledding hill for the people of Milford.

W.L. Lovejoy is the name over the door, one of the many proprietors of this carriage trimming, harness, and wheelwright shop on Elm Street. In 1898, Isaac Brothers expanded the services to include bicycle repairing. It was purchased by the Sons of Veterans in 1911 and was known as the Armory. Several organizations rented the space and used it for military drills, lodge meetings, dances, and parties. The Granite Grange bought it in 1921, and it burned down in 1926.

Edward Shaughnessey (far left), an Irish immigrant, stands in front of his wheelwright shop on the south side of the Oval. He operated the business from 1873 until the building was moved to Smith Street in 1903. The large building in the center was a blacksmith shop, originally constructed by Jonathan Buxton in 1797. In 1943, the blacksmith shop was razed, and the site became a memorial for the 13 Milford men who gave their lives in World War II.

CHAPTER 6

SCHOOLS

Located at the intersection of Foster Road and Federal Hill Road, this schoolhouse, built in 1897, was the third schoolhouse on this site. An average of 16 students received their education in this building. It closed in 1924 because there were not enough students to justify it staying open. Today, it is a private residence.

When Centennial High School opened in August 1895, the *Farmer's Cabinet* called it "A handsome brick and granite structure. Interior arrangements afford every convenience for teachers and scholars. Finest location in town." The building served as Milford's high school until 1961. Eight years later, in 1969, it was renamed Bales Elementary School in honor of longtime school superintendent Harold C. Bales. The opening of Heron Pond Elementary School in 2001 brought an end to elementary classes at Bales.

Population growth has always been a challenge for school administrators in Milford. Milford Middle School was approved in 1968, built in 1969, and open in January 1970 with students from Amherst and Milford as part of the AREA agreement. After Milford and Amherst school boards voted in June 1973, Amherst seventh graders exited back to Amherst in 1974 and eighth graders in 1975. The middle school underwent a $5-million expansion in 1992 to again accommodate additional students.

The District No. 9 School, also known as the West Primary and Grammar but best known as the "Old White," was built in 1860. One resident recalled it was a common prank on July 3 for students to ring the school's bell. The building became expensive to maintain, and in 1924, the town voted to demolish it and erect a larger brick structure. The Milford Police Station was built on the former school site in 2006.

Garden Street School, seen in the above image, was built in 1925 and replaced the Old White School, which was previously in this spot. Garden Street served as a grammar and elementary school for 77 years. Milford High School's class of 2013 was the final class to go to first grade here. Milford's police station was built on the site of the school and opened in September 2006 after 18 months of construction.

From 1853 to 1926, this building, often called "the Old Brick," served as a school. In 1929, John T. Smith used the building to manufacture curtains and for storage. From 1946 to 1950, Textron Inc. leased the building. Textron specifically chose small communities for its textile manufacturing and employed approximately 150 people. The Cabinet Press moved its operations here in 1950. The above photograph, taken in the 1940s, shows the building before an addition was constructed in 1968.

This building was erected in 1911 to replace the original school, which burned down on Christmas Day 1910. Located on Elm Street close to the Wilton town line, it was attended by children of Pine Valley Mill workers. The school closed in 1942, and it became a private residence. For many years, it was used as a day care center until it was razed in 2014 to make room for a Dunkin' Donuts parking lot.

Discover Thousands of Local History Books Featuring Millions of Vintage Images

Arcadia Publishing, the leading local history publisher in the United States, is committed to making history accessible and meaningful through publishing books that celebrate and preserve the heritage of America's people and places.

Find more books like this at
www.arcadiapublishing.com

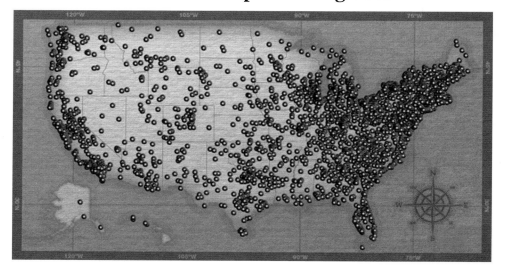

Search for your hometown history, your old stomping grounds, and even your favorite sports team.